D0556128

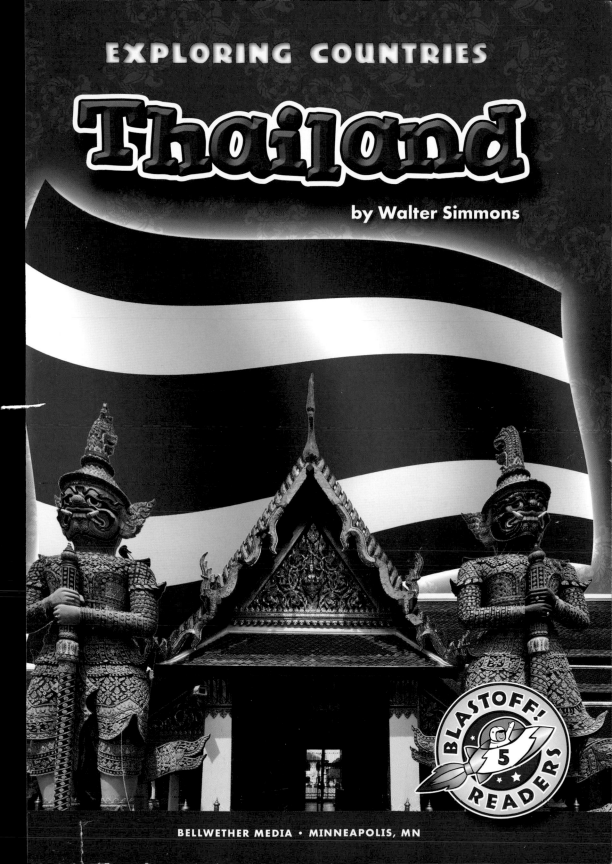

EXPLORING COUNTRIES

Thailand

by Walter Simmons

BELLWETHER MEDIA • MINNEAPOLIS, MN

Note to Librarians, Teachers, and Parents:

Blastoff! Readers are carefully developed by literacy experts and combine standards-based content with developmentally appropriate text.

Level 1 provides the most support through repetition of high-frequency words, light text, predictable sentence patterns, and strong visual support.

Level 2 offers early readers a bit more challenge through varied simple sentences, increased text load, and less repetition of high-frequency words.

Level 3 advances early-fluent readers toward fluency through increased text and concept load, less reliance on visuals, longer sentences, and more literary language.

Level 4 builds reading stamina by providing more text per page, increased use of punctuation, greater variation in sentence patterns, and increasingly challenging vocabulary.

Level 5 encourages children to move from "learning to read" to "reading to learn" by providing even more text, varied writing styles, and less familiar topics.

Whichever book is right for your reader, Blastoff! Readers are the perfect books to build confidence and encourage a love of reading that will last a lifetime!

This edition first published in 2011 by Bellwether Media, Inc.

No part of this publication may be reproduced in whole or in part without written permission of the publisher. For information regarding permission, write to Bellwether Media, Inc., Attention: Permissions Department, 5357 Penn Avenue South, Minneapolis, MN 55419.

Library of Congress Cataloging-in-Publication Data

Contents

Myanmar

Laos

Thailand

Bangkok

Andaman
Sea

Cambodia

Gulf of
Thailand

Phuket

Malaysia

Thailand is a country in Southeast Asia that covers 198,117 square miles (513,120 square kilometers). It borders Myanmar to the west, Laos to the north and east, and Cambodia to the southeast. The capital of Thailand is Bangkok.

Thailand extends south along the Malay **Peninsula**. This narrow stretch of land includes Thailand's southern neighbor, Malaysia. To the west of the peninsula is the Andaman Sea, and to the east is the **Gulf** of Thailand. Several large islands lie off the coasts of Thailand. The largest of these islands is Phuket, in the Andaman Sea.

Thailand has many different landscapes. There are **fertile** plains, high **plateaus**, and steep mountain ranges. Much of northeastern Thailand is covered by the Khorat Plateau. Thais also call this region *Isan*. The Phetchabun Mountains separate *Isan* from the central plains. The Tenasserim Mountains run along Thailand's border with Myanmar. In the north, steep hills rise to Doi Inthanon, the highest point in Thailand. In the south, Thailand and Myanmar share the narrow **Isthmus** of Kra.

Two major river systems, the Chao Phraya and the Mekong, flow through Thailand. Many **tributaries** that flow into Thailand join the Mekong on its way to the South China Sea.

fun fact

The shallow waters along Thailand's coasts offer some of the best snorkeling in the world. Thousands of people come to Thailand to snorkel every year.

The wide Chao Phraya River, joined by its tributaries, flows through the center of Thailand. Along its banks are small towns, narrow roads, and rice farms. The river grows wider as it passes through the middle of Bangkok and empties into the Bay of Bangkok. Water taxis and riverboats carry passengers up and down the river. For many people, this is the fastest way to get around Bangkok.

Wat Phra Kaew stands near the river. This temple holds a statue called the Emerald Buddha, an important religious **artifact** made of green **jasper** and gold. Near Wat Phra Kaew is the Grand Palace. This palace has been home to many kings of Thailand.

Emerald Buddha

fun fact

The Emerald Buddha has three different suits of gold clothing. At the change of every season, the king of Thailand changes the statue's suit.

king cobra

Did you know?

One of the most dangerous animals in Thailand is the king cobra, which can grow to be 18 feet (5.5 meters) long. The king cobra kills its prey with deadly venom.

! fun fact

The Siamese cat is native to Thailand, which was once known as the Kingdom of Siam.

Mammals, birds, and fish thrive in Thailand. The country has many **sanctuaries** that protect wildlife. Gibbons and macaques swing through forest treetops while tigers, clouded leopards, and sun bears chase their prey across the forest floor. Another forest animal, the barking deer, is named for the barking sound it makes when it senses danger. The binturong, sometimes called the Asian bearcat, lives in trees and eats fruits and insects. Some Thais keep binturongs as pets.

binturong

macaque

dugong

Carp, catfish, eels, and the poisonous grunting toadfish lurk in Thailand's rivers. Dolphins, sea turtles, and dugongs swim in the coastal waters along the Andaman Sea. Dugongs live in groups. Some people call them sea cows because they graze on sea grasses. Cranes and storks nest along the coasts. Many different kinds of birds **migrate** through Thailand.

Thailand has about 66 million people. Most Thais live in the central region of the country and have **ancestors** who lived in and around Thailand. The country is also home to people with roots in Laos, Vietnam, and China. A few groups, including the Hmong, live in the hills and mountains of Thailand. Southern Thailand is home to the Yawi people. Most of the Yawi people follow the Islamic faith. Both the Hmong and the Yawi have their own cultures and traditions.

Speak Thai!

English	Thai	How to say it
hello	sawat dee	sawat DEE
good-bye	la korn	LAH gone
yes	châi	chai
no	mâi chai	MAI chai
please	dâi bproht	DAI bproht
thank you	korb khun	KOP kun
friend	pêuan	PU-an

Did you know?

About nine out of ten Thais follow the Buddhist religion. They pay regular visits to *wats*. In these temples, they make offerings and pray in front of statues of Buddha.

Many languages are spoken in Thailand. Thai is the country's official language, but Chinese, Vietnamese, and Lao can also be heard in the country. The Hmong, Yawi, and other groups often speak their own languages.

floating market

In Thai cities, people live in apartments and small houses. People usually take buses or ride motorbikes to get from place to place. In Bangkok, the Skytrain glides along elevated tracks around the city. To get to surrounding islands, people use large ferries that can carry vehicles. People visit shops, malls, and street markets. Many shop at floating markets, where fruits, flowers, and other goods are sold from boats in Thailand's rivers. The largest floating market is Damnoen Saduak in Bangkok.

Where People Live in Thailand

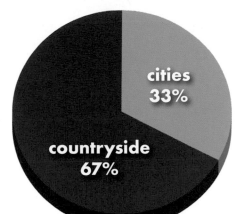

cities
33%

countryside
67%

In the countryside, farmers live in villages and small towns. They walk or drive to their **rice paddies** and **pastures**. A Thai country home usually has an open patio on the ground floor and sleeping rooms upstairs.

fun fact

Houses on the banks of rivers throughout Thailand need to be built on stilts. If they are not, they will fill with water when the rivers flood!

Thai children must go to school for nine years, starting at age 6. They go to elementary school for six years. There, they learn Thai, math, science, art, technology, social studies, and physical education. Students must then attend three years of high school, or *mathayom*.

They may continue with high school for three more years, or go to a school that teaches them job skills. To enter a university, Thai students must complete *mathayom* and take a series of tests. High scores allow them to attend a university. The biggest universities are in Bangkok and the northern city of Chiang Mai.

Did you know?

After finishing school, many Thai boys spend a year as a monk. They have their heads shaved and dress in robes of saffron, a bright orange color. They learn about the Buddhist religion and must eat only what is offered to them by generous Thai people.

Thais work in many different industries. In the cities, people work in factories that make cars, computers, appliances, clothing, and furniture. Many Thais have **service jobs**. They work in shops, hotels, restaurants, banks, and other businesses. They also serve people from around the world who come to visit Thailand's cities, landmarks, and beach resorts.

Did you know?
Thailand has one of the world's largest populations of working elephants. They move heavy logs, stones, and equipment for construction projects.

In the countryside, many people raise crops and livestock. Landowners hire seasonal workers to tend the rice crop. They plant rice during the rainy season in late spring. The rice is harvested late in the year.

Where People Work in Thailand

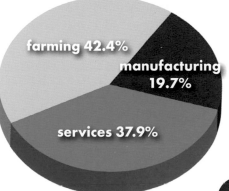

farming 42.4%

manufacturing 19.7%

services 37.9%

Muay Thai

Thais enjoy spending their free time with friends and family. They often gather in large groups to visit shops, restaurants, and markets. Thais also love to watch and play sports. In Thailand, soccer is a favorite sport for kids. Muay Thai is a kind of kickboxing that is popular throughout the country. It is also called the "Art of Eight Limbs" because fighters use their hands, elbows, knees, and feet to strike each other.

Thailand's natural landscapes offer plenty of other activities. Snorkeling and scuba diving are popular along the seacoasts. Hikers explore the hills and mountains. Thais can spend several days outdoors hiking in small groups from one campsite to the next.

! fun fact

In *takraw*, two teams try to keep a small ball in the air with their feet or legs. *Takraw* is like hacky sack with a volleyball net.

takraw

fun fact

In any big Thai food market, customers crowd around the insect stands. Cooks fry grasshoppers, crickets, caterpillars, cockroaches, and worms in big skillets and sell them to customers.

Thai people love spicy food. They use many different kinds of chilies to add flavor and heat to their dishes. Curry is a favorite dish. It is a spicy stew made with beef, chicken, or shrimp. Thai cooks flavor their food with coconut milk or a splash of lime juice. Rice is served with nearly every meal in Thailand. Jasmine rice has a slightly sweet and nutty flavor. Sticky rice is a variety grown in the northeast. People use their hands to form small balls of sticky rice, which they eat with any kind of food.

In the cities, many people dine at sidewalk tables or roadside stands. Vendors sell hot soup, fried rice, noodle dishes, and grilled meats. Thais can also buy sliced fruit, fresh coconut, juice, or ice cream.

sticky rice

green curry

Thailand has many national and religious holidays. Chakri Day happens on April 6. This day celebrates the founding of the city of Bangkok and the Chakri **dynasty**, the royal family of Thailand. On August 12, Thais celebrate the birthday of Queen Sirikit, the current queen of Thailand. This is also celebrated as Mother's Day. Chulalongkorn Day on October 23 honors King Chulalongkorn, who ruled Thailand from 1868 to 1910. All over Thailand, people lay wreaths on statues of this famous king.

Songkran takes place in the middle of April. This is the start of the New Year according to the Buddhist calendar. By tradition, this is the time to wash away the troubles of the past year. People line the streets with water pistols and buckets. They splash each other and everyone who walks by.

Songkran

Portraits of King Bhumibol Adulyadej are everywhere in Thailand. His image can be seen in train stations, shops, and on the walls of buildings. The Thai people have deep respect for their king. He is often seen in yellow shirts, robes, and suits. Yellow is the traditional color of the Thai **monarchy**. Many Thai people wear yellow to show their love for the king. To Thais, the king is a symbol of Thailand's proud history as an independent nation.

King
Bhumibol Adulyadej

fun fact

King Bhumibol Adulyadej lives in Chitralada Palace. However, the king isn't its only resident. The royal white elephants also live on the palace grounds!

Fast Facts About Thailand

Thailand's Flag

The Thai flag has five horizontal bands. The middle band is blue and sits between two bands of white. The bands at the top and bottom are red. The blue band stands for the king and is twice as wide as the other bands. The red bands stand for the nation of Thailand, and the white for the religion of Buddhism. This flag, officially adopted in 1917, often flies alongside a yellow flag that shows the emblem of the king.

Official Name: Kingdom of Thailand

Area: 198,117 square miles (513,120 square kilometers); Thailand is the 50th largest country in the world.

Capital City:	Bangkok
Important Cities:	Nonthaburi, Hat Yai, Chiang Mai
Population:	66,404,688 (July 2010)
Official Language:	Thai
National Holiday:	His Majesty the King's Birthday (December 5); the date changes whenever a new king is crowned.
Religions:	Buddhist (95%), Muslim (5%)
Major Industries:	farming, fishing, manufacturing, services, tourism
Natural Resources:	natural gas, oil, rubber, tin
Manufactured Products:	cars, cement, computers, clothing, electronics, furniture
Farm Products:	rice, cashews, citrus fruits, coconuts, corn, eucalyptus, potatoes, soybeans
Unit of Money:	baht; the baht is divided into 100 satang.

Glossary

ancestors—relatives who lived long ago

artifact—a man-made item from long ago that is important to people today

dynasty—a group of rulers from one family line

fertile—supports growth

gulf—part of an ocean that extends into land

isthmus—a narrow strip of land that lies between two bodies of water; an isthmus connects two larger pieces of land.

jasper—a blackish green stone

migrate—to move from one place to another, often with the seasons

monarchy—a form of government where one person, often a king or queen, rules the nation

pastures—areas where livestock graze

peninsula—a section of land that extends out from a larger piece of land and is almost completely surrounded by water

plateaus—areas of flat, raised land

rice paddies—fields that are flooded with water and used to grow rice

sanctuaries—protected areas; Thailand has many sanctuaries to protect its wildlife.

service jobs—jobs that perform tasks for people or businesses

tributaries—streams or rivers that flow into a larger stream or river

To Learn More

AT THE LIBRARY
Campbell, Geoffrey A. *Thailand*. San Diego, Calif.:
Lucent Books, 2002.

Friedman, Mel. *Thailand*. New York, N.Y.:
Children's Press, 2009.

Taus-Bolstad, Stacy. *Thailand in Pictures*.
Minneapolis, Minn.: Lerner Publications, 2004.

ON THE WEB
Learning more about Thailand
is as easy as 1, 2, 3.

1. Go to www.factsurfer.com.

2. Enter "Thailand" into the search box.

3. Click the "Surf" button and you will see a list of
   related Web sites.

With factsurfer.com, finding more information is just
a click away.

Index

The images in this book are reproduced through the courtesy of: Juan Martinez, front cover, pp. 6-7, 9 (small), 23 (top); Maisei Raman, front cover (flag), p. 28; Jon Eppard, pp. 4-5; Christophe Schmid, p. 7 (small); Alan Copson/Photolibrary, p. 8; Ruth Tomlinson/Photolibrary, p. 9; Indiapicture/Alamy, pp. 10-11; Getty Images, pp. 11 (top), 24; Pangfolio.com, p. 11 (middle); Wolfgang Poezier/Photolibrary, p. 11 (bottom); Walter G Allgower/Photolibrary, pp. 12, 15; Juriah Mosin, p. 14; Kevin O'Hara/Age Fotostock, p. 16; DOZIER Marc/Photolibrary, p. 17; Neil Bowman/Age Fotostock, pp. 18-19; Gavin Hellier/Photolibrary, p. 20; Jochen Tack/Photolibrary, p. 21; Laurie Noble/Getty Images, p. 22; Alistair Michael Thomas, p. 23 (bottom); AFP/Getty Images, pp. 25, 26 (small); Associated Press/AP Images, pp. 26-27; Bloomberg/Getty Images, p. 27 (small); Lim ChewHow, p. 29 (bill & coin).